FROM SLAVE TO SOLDIER

BASED ON A TRUE CIVIL WAR STORY

BY **DEBORAH HOPKINSON**
ILLUSTRATED BY **BRIAN FLOCA**

READY–TO–READ
ALADDIN
NEW YORK LONDON TORONTO SYDNEY

For Ellie and Nick
—D. H.

For Teresa Genaro, with thanks
for the Volkswagen
—B. F.

🦜 ALADDIN PAPERBACKS
An imprint of Simon & Schuster Children's Publishing Division
1230 Avenue of the Americas, New York, NY 10020
Text copyright © 2005 by Deborah Hopkinson
Illustrations copyright © 2005 by Brian Floca
All rights reserved, including the right of reproduction in whole or in part in any form.
READY-TO-READ is a registered trademark of Simon & Schuster, Inc.
ALADDIN PAPERBACKS and colophon are trademarks of Simon & Schuster, Inc.
Also available in an Atheneum Books for Young Readers hardcover edition.
Designed by Abelardo Martínez
The text of this book was set in Century Old Style.
The illustrations were rendered in watercolors.
Manufactured in the United States of America
First Aladdin Paperbacks edition January 2007
10 9 8 7

The Library of Congress has cataloged the hardcover edition as follows:
Hopkinson, Deborah.
From slave to soldier : based on a true Civil War story /
Deborah Hopkinson ; illustrated by Brian Floca.—1st ed.
p.   cm.
Summary: A boy who hates being a slave joins the Union Army to fight for freedom, and proves himself brave and capable of handling a mule team when the need arises.
[1. Slavery—Fiction. 2. Soldiers—Fiction. 3. African Americans—Fiction. 4. Drovers—Fiction.
5. Mules—Fiction. 6. United States—History—Civil War, 1861–1865—Fiction.] I. Floca, Brian, ill. II.
Title.
PZ7.H778125Fr 2005
[Fic]—dc22
2004026933
ISBN-13: 978-0-689-83965-8 (hc.)
ISBN-10: 0-689-83965-0 (hc.)
ISBN-13: 978-0-689-83966-5 (pbk.)
ISBN-10: 0-689-83966-9 (pbk.)
0217 LAK

Contents

Johnny and Nell

Johnny was a small boy, but each
morning he got on Nell's back and drove
forty cows into their milking pens.

Later Johnny helped to churn the butter, carried buckets of water from the spring, and rode Nell to the fields to bring the men lunch. He worked hard all day long, but no one ever thanked him.

Instead, when one of the cows wandered away, the mistress gave Johnny a beating.

Johnny put his head against Nell's neck and wiped away a tear. "Oh, Nell, even when I try my best, they don't care," he whispered. "Now that Mama's gone, you and Uncle Silas are all I have. I love you, girl. But I sure hate being a slave."

Uncle Silas longed for freedom too.

"Folks in the Southern states want to keep us in slavery, but Abe Lincoln aims to set us free," Uncle Silas told Johnny.

"Would you fight if there is a war?" Johnny asked.

Uncle Silas said softly, "I'm too old to be a soldier, Johnny. But if I was young like you, I just might join the Union army!"

Soldiers!

One cold day Johnny and Nell were
driving the cows to a pasture near the
road. Suddenly Nell let out a loud snort.

Johnny saw hundreds of soldiers
marching toward them. "Look at their
blue uniforms," he whispered into Nell's
ear. "Those are Union soldiers from
the North."

A tall soldier left the line and came up to Johnny. "Hello there. My name is Ben. Is this fine black mule yours?"

"No, sir," said Johnny. "She belongs to Dr. Hogatt. This is his farm. I'm a slave here."

"Is that so?" said Ben, scratching Nell's soft nose. "Well, since it's not your farm and not your mule, why don't you come along with us? We could use a strong boy like you. You can join the Union army and be free."

The Union army wanted him! Johnny could hardly believe his ears. He looked into the soldier's kind face. "But if I go, I'll be a runaway."

Ben patted his shoulder. "Don't worry, we'll take care of you."

Johnny didn't want to be a slave. But how could he leave Uncle Silas and Nell? Then he remembered what Uncle Silas had said. Johnny made up his mind. "If I join the Union army, maybe I can help Uncle Silas get free too."

Johnny threw his arms around Nell's neck. Nell nudged his arm with her big head. "You must go home now," he told her. "But I'll never forget you, girl."

Then Johnny fell into step beside his new friend. Ben smiled. "This here's Johnny," he told the others. "He wants to be a soldier."

The Long March

At first Johnny felt excited as he walked along. But the soldiers marched so fast, he could hardly keep up. His feet began to hurt. He felt small and shy.

He missed Uncle Silas and Nell. *Do I really belong here?* he wondered. But it was too late. He couldn't turn back now.

When the soldiers stopped, everybody got busy making camp. Johnny stood alone, wondering what to do.

Ben took his arm. "Come and meet Dave. He drives the supply wagon. You can help him feed the mules."

At suppertime Dave gave Johnny a
tin plate and a cup. Johnny ate stew and
a biscuit called hardtack. Everything
tasted strange and new.

After supper the soldiers told stories around the fire. "Come sit by me, little Johnny," said Dave. At bedtime Dave spread out a blanket. "Roll up in this to stay warm," he said.

Johnny tried to sleep on the cold, hard ground. His legs were sore. His heart was sore too. *Did I do the right thing?* Johnny wondered.

In the Union Army

Dave woke Johnny with a gentle shake. "I'm taking you to meet the captain this morning," Dave said. "He's in charge of Company C."

When they entered the tent, Dave saluted. "Captain, this is Johnny," said Dave, patting Johnny's shoulder. "He's the boy we picked up on the road."

The captain said, "So, you want to be a soldier. You're a little young, aren't you?"

Johnny was scared, but he lifted his chin. "I'm small but I'm strong. I can take care of a mule."

"That's the spirit," said the captain with a smile.

"I could use help with the supply wagon," Dave said.

The captain nodded. "Want to give it a try, Johnny?"

Johnny tried to salute just like Dave. "Oh yes, sir!"

Dave and the captain grinned.

Dave was proud of his mules. "Our team is the best," he told Johnny. "Here are Jimmy and Jenny, the lead mules. Pete and Rhoda pull in the middle, and Kitty and Tuff are closest to the wagon wheels."

Johnny scratched Kitty's neck. She looked just like Nell. "It's not easy to drive a team of six mules," Dave warned him.

Johnny smiled and patted Kitty. "I'm ready to try."

Count on Johnny!

Every day Johnny worked hard at driving
the team. "You're good with the mules,"
Dave told him.

"Can I drive the team alone?"
Johnny asked eagerly.

"Whoa, not so fast," said Dave.
"You're not ready just yet."

One night Dave did not join the others at supper. The captain asked, "Where's Dave?"

"He has a bad stomachache," said Johnny.

The captain frowned. "What's in your wagon, Johnny?"

"Bacon, coffee, and hardtack," Johnny told him.

The captain looked worried. "Some of our soldiers are keeping watch down the road. They haven't eaten since morning," he said.

"Let me drive the wagon to them," Johnny begged.

"Can you handle the mules alone, Johnny?" asked the captain.

Johnny swallowed hard. "You can count on me."

It was hard to hitch up the mules in the dark, but Johnny did it. He gave Kitty an extra pat. "Ben and the other soldiers are hungry," he told her. "They need us to bring them food. Let's prove that we can do it."

Johnny drove the wagon down the dark road. Now and then, the moon peeked out from behind the clouds. Johnny shivered in the cold air. Suddenly he heard rushing water. Up ahead he could see a bridge. Oh no! A river!

On the Bridge

The roar of the water filled Johnny's
ears. Johnny was afraid to cross the
bridge. But what else could he do? Ben
and the other soldiers needed him! "Let's
go, team!" he called.

Slowly the mules lifted their heavy
feet onto the wooden planks. Johnny tried
not to look down. Just thinking about
that deep, cold water made him shiver.

Boom! A cannon roared close by.
The mules shuddered and tossed their
heads. Their eyes were wide with fear.

Johnny tried to calm his team. "Steady now." Suddenly he felt an awful jolt. *Crack!* "What was that?" cried Johnny.

He felt the wagon jerk. One of the wheels had broken through a plank in the bridge!

Johnny looked down. If the wagon slipped more, they would all topple into the rushing river. He tightened Kitty's reins and kicked her sides hard. "Let's go, Kitty!"

Johnny felt Kitty pulling, but the heavy wagon didn't move. Johnny leaned down and yelled, "Come on, girl! You can do it."

Slowly, slowly Johnny felt the wagon lift up. There! The wheel was free at last. They moved across the bridge to safety.

Kitty's sides were shaking. Johnny's hands were shaking too. In the moonlight he saw soldiers up ahead. Suddenly he heard someone call out, "Look, fellows! It's Johnny."

Ben rushed to the wagon and lifted Johnny down. "Are you okay, Ben?" asked Johnny.

"Thanks to you we are," said Ben with a grin.

"Hooray for Johnny!" the men cried in low, excited whispers.

The Littlest Mule-Team Driver

The next morning Dave felt better.
Johnny and Dave were fixing their wagon
when the captain came to see them. "Is this
the wagon of the best mule-team drivers
in the Union army?" he asked.

Dave put his arm around Johnny. "It sure is, sir. I didn't think Johnny was ready. But he proved he could drive a team as well as any soldier."

The captain nodded. "There's only one problem."

"Did I do something wrong, sir?" Johnny was worried.

"No, the problem is that you don't look like a soldier," the captain said.

Johnny glanced down at his ragged clothes. "But this is all I have," he said. The captain winked and handed him a bundle. Johnny tore it open. "A uniform! Oh, thank you."

The captain shook Johnny's hand. "Thank *you*, Johnny. We're proud to have such a brave boy in Company C."

Johnny beamed. "I'm proud to be here, sir." Johnny put on his new coat and cap and saluted. Dave and the captain saluted back.

Johnny ran to show Kitty his new uniform. "Look, girl! I really do belong now. I just wish Uncle Silas and Nell could see me." Kitty nudged his arm with her big head, just like Nell used to do.

"I love you, Kitty," Johnny said as he laughed. "And my new friends, too. But most of all I love being free."

Author's Note

During the Civil War, African Americans struggled to be accepted as soldiers. *From Slave to Soldier* is fiction, but it is based on the true story of a boy named John McCline, who was enslaved on a Tennessee plantation until the age of eleven. One day in 1862 he ran away and joined a passing group of Union soldiers in the Thirteenth Michigan Infantry Regiment. Young John became a mule-team driver's helper in the Union army until the end of the Civil War.

After the war John went to school and worked in hotels. In 1892 he went to work for the family of Herbert Hagerman and moved to Santa Fe, New Mexico. Around 1930 McCline showed his handwritten memoir of his early years to Hagerman, who typed it and wrote an introduction. Although it did not become a book during McCline's life, the typed copy was kept in his family and published by the University of Tennessee Press in 1998.[*] McCline married at age eighty-six and died in 1948, when he was about ninety-five.

This story is based on McCline's memory of driving a wagon alone to bring supplies to the battlefield. Years after his war experiences McCline remembered the names of all his mules, and they have not been changed in this story. Many blacks in the Union army were not treated as kindly as young McCline was. But John McCline's incredible memory for detail helps us better understand what life was like for one boy who went from being "a slave to a soldier." I hope that someday you will read his book.

*Furman, Jan, ed. *Slavery in the Clover Bottoms: John McCline's Narrative of His Life During Slavery and the Civil War.* Voices of the Civil War Series. Knoxville: University of Tennessee Press, 1998.